D1093236

PRESENTED TO:

_____

FROM:

_____

DATE:

_____

You're so blessed
among women,
And the babe
in your womb,
also blessed!

LUKE 1:42
THE MESSAGE

WHAT A WONDERFUL LiFe

For Moms

Standard
PUBLISHING
Bringing The Word to Life

Published by Standard Publishing
Cincinnati, Ohio
A division of Standex International Corporation
Printed in China
© Copyright 2005 Mark Gilroy Communications, Inc.
6528 E. 101st Street, Suite 416
Tulsa, Oklahoma 74133
www.markgilroy.com

Designed and illustrated by jacksondesignco, LLC
Springdale, Arkansas
www.jacksondesignco.com

ISBN 0-7847-1798-2

Acknowledgments

Nancy B. Gibbs wrote "In My Steps" on page 23,
"Wildflowers" on page 65, and "Never Alone" on page 79.

Christy Philippe wrote "The Extra Mile" on page 37, "A Real Home" on
page 51, "Family Portraits" on page 60, and "God's Light" on page 89.

"My Greatest Achievement" on page 74 is adapted from
message boards by mothers at www.heinzforbaby.com/au.

We found "Kids Say" on pages 28-29 and 42 in several places without
attribution. Every effort was made to track down an original author. If you
know where this material originated, we'd love it if you would contact us.

Table of Contents

Let the thankful heart sweep through the day and, as the magnet finds the iron, so it will find, in every hour, some heavenly blessing.

HENRY WARD BEECHER

Introduction

A mother's best gift to her children—and to herself—is her attitude of gratitude.

How often do you stop to think about how wonderful your life really is? Do you believe in your heart that life really is good?

No single attitude will change your outlook on life more profoundly and quickly than simple gratitude. A thankful heart is a joyful heart, because even in the middle of challenges—children squabbling, not enough money in the checkbook, driving kids to soccer practice and everywhere in between, your own needs and feelings of fatigue—gratitude realizes that God's world is full of blessings and miracles—including your children and you!

As you read the following pages, let your heart and attitude be changed by a new sense of wonder that comes when you view life through the eyes of gratitude, optimism, and most importantly, faith in a loving God.

God looked over everything he had made; it was so good, so very good!

GENESIS 1:31 THE MESSAGE

When I first open my eyes upon the morning meadows and look out upon the beautiful world, I thank God I am alive.

RALPH WALDO EMERSON

WHAT A WONDERFUL WORLD

LIFE IS WONDERFUL BECAUSE HE PUT THE STARS IN THE SKY—AND HE CREATED A WONDERFUL CHILD INSIDE OF YOU.

The Miracle of Life

Babies are such a nice way to start people.

DON HERROLD

God is an amazing creator. Perhaps nothing shows it more beautifully than the way he creates a newborn baby.

Your child started out as one little cell, a bundle of potential. By three weeks after conception, the cell had multiplied, and the structure of basic organs and fundamental body shape began forming.

By four weeks, his heart was beating.

By seven weeks, your baby was moving on his own, and had developed tiny fingers, toes, and eyes.

By eight weeks, your child had grown to about an inch and a half and had all her organs. Her development was exploding—she grew about 100,000 nerve cells every minute.

By eleven weeks, all bodily systems were working. He could jump, grasp, hiccup, dream, hear, and feel.

By four months, she could make facial expressions. By four and a half months, he responded to a touch on his lips by sucking, just like a newborn baby.

By seven months, your baby could open his eyes. He began to process and respond to light and sound.

By nine months, your child's brain was fully formed, functioning much like a newborn's. Most of her bones had hardened. The hair on her head had thickened and become coarser. Her lungs were mature and capable of taking in air. She was ready to be born.

> *You made all the delicate, inner parts of my body*
> *and knit me together in my mother's womb.*
>
> PSALM 139:13 NLT

A Perfect World

The more I study nature the more I am amazed at the Creator.

LOUIS PASTEUR

Life is truly wonderful because of the world that God created for
us to inhabit.

The earth is tilted at 23.45 degrees—the perfect angle to support
life. Without the tilt to deflect the light and heat, the earth
would become too hot and water would build up in the north
and south poles.

The earth travels around the sun in an elliptical orbit at a
fairly constant speed. If our world slowed down, it would be
pulled so close to the sun at the narrow part of the orbit that
the earth would burn. If the earth orbited slightly more than
twice as fast as it does, it would break free from its orbit,
freezing us to death.

If the mass of our earth were only one-fourth less than it is, our atmosphere would be less dense and most of the planet would be an icy wasteland.

If the earth's crust were only ten feet thicker all the way around, the atmosphere would have less free oxygen, and life could not have begun.

If the earth were just 5% closer to the Sun, the increased heat would melt the polar ice caps, raising the water level by as much as 300 feet.

If the earth rotated every 36 hours instead of every 24 hours, the temperature would roller coaster throughout the day, making life very uncomfortable, if not impossible.

Look at the night skies: Who do you think made all this?
Who marches this army of stars out each night,
counts them off, calls each by name—so magnificent!
so powerful!—and never overlooks a single one?

ISAIAH 40:26 THE MESSAGE

To Do!
A Walk in the Woods

To rekindle a sense of awe and wonder for God's wonderful world in your children's lives—and in your own life—plan a walk in the woods. You obviously need to consider the ages of your children when determining the kind of terrain you will explore and the distance of your walk. But get as far away from the ordinary as you can on a day trip. If your children are younger, provide them with a bag to "collect" things that interest them. They will love this part of your activity even if all they pick up are twigs and rocks. For older children and teens (and yourself) supply a journal and toward the end of the day set aside time to write down impressions of God's creation—and a prayer of thanksgiving to God for the world he has made.

Take time to marvel at the wonders of life.

GARY W. FENCHUK

God's World

O World, I cannot hold thee close enough!
Thy winds, thy wide gray skies!
Thy mists that roll and rise!
Thy woods, this autumn day, that ache and sag
And all but cry with color! That gaunt crag
To crush! To lift the lean of that black bluff!
World, World, I cannot get thee close enough!

Long have I known a glory in it all,
But never knew I this;
Here such a passion is
As stretcheth me apart. Lord, I do fear
Thou hast made the world too beautiful this year.
My soul is all but out of me—let fall
No burning leaf; prithee, let no bird call.

EDNA ST. VINCENT MILLAY

LORD, you have created such a beautiful world. Just looking at a night sky, I'm amazed by the distance and beauty of the stars—the magnitude of your beautiful creation. Help me see your work anew today, God. Quicken my adoration for your creativity and might. Help me give my children a sense of awe of you, Lord God. Thank you for the wonderful world you've given us to live in.

*Her children respect
and bless her; her husband
joins in with words of praise.*

PROVERBS 31:28 THE MESSAGE

A mother
is a mother still,
The holiest
thing alive.

SAMUEL TAYLOR COLERIDGE

WHAT A WONDERFUL YOU

GOD MADE YOU—AND YOUR CHILDREN—
UNIQUE AND SPECIAL. NEVER FORGET
HOW MUCH YOU ARE LOVED.

Mother is the name for God in the lips and hearts of little children.

WILLIAM MAKEPEACE THACKERAY

In My Steps

My four-year-old son was on my heels no matter where I went. Whenever I stopped to do something and turned back around, I would trip over him.

I patiently suggested fun activities to keep him occupied. But he simply smiled an innocent smile and said, "Oh, that's all right, Mommy. I'd rather be in here with you." Then he continued to bounce happily along behind me.

After stepping on his toes for the fifth time, I began to lose patience.

When I asked him why he was acting this way, he looked up at me with sweet green eyes and said, "Well, Mommy, my Sunday school teacher told me to walk in Jesus' footsteps. I can't see him, so I'm walking in yours!"

And you should follow my example, just as I follow Christ's.

1 CORINTHIANS 11:1 NLT

Caring for Your Soul

A mother's day is demanding. In the daily busyness of fixing meals, dispensing wisdom, doing laundry, and helping kids with homework, it's easy to lose a sense of purpose.

As easy as it is to care for your children at the expense of caring for yourself, you enrich your life as a mother when you remember that your mothering work begins with yourself. To know and meet your children's needs, you must know and meet your own needs. To raise children that sparkle and sing, you must express your own gifts. To teach your children to relish life, you must find and express your own joy.

As you allow God's love for you to enable you to love yourself, your love with overflow freely into your children's lives—and you'll find and fulfill your purpose as a mother.

Jesus commands us to treat others as we would have them treat us. You'll find that it is impossible to love your children as richly as you'd like to without first loving yourself.

God's love is not
a conditional love;
it is an open-hearted,
generous self-giving
which God offers to men.

J.B. PHILLIPS

*We know how dearly God
loves us, because he has
given us the Holy Spirit to fill
our hearts with his love.*

ROMANS 5:5 NLT

25

A Wonderful Hair Day

God knows you inside and out. The Bible says that God knows you so well that he has even counted the number of hairs on your head! Scientists say that there are approximately 100,000 hairs on the human head—give or take the 100 or so we lose each day. That's a lot of counting!

God cares so much for you that he wants to know everything about you. You are unique and special—because he created you that way! Never forget that every part of you—even the hairs on your head—are wonderful in his eyes.

Not even a sparrow,
worth only half a penny,
can fall to the ground without
your Father knowing it. And the
very hairs on your head are all
numbered. So don't be afraid;
you are more valuable to
him than a whole flock
of sparrows.

MATTHEW 10:29–31 NLT

27

Kids Say

Life is wonderful because of the
innocence and honesty of children...

HOW DID GOD MAKE MOTHERS?

- He used dirt, just like for the rest of us.
- Magic plus super powers and a lot of stirring.
- God made my mom just the same like he made me.
- He just used bigger parts.

WHAT INGREDIENTS ARE MOTHERS MADE OF?

- God makes mothers out of clouds and angel hair and everything nice in the world and one dab of mean.
- They had to get their start from men's bones.
- Then they mostly use string, I think.

WHAT KIND OF LITTLE GIRL WAS YOUR MOM?

- My mom has always been my mom and none of that other stuff.

- I don't know because I wasn't there, but my guess would be pretty bossy.

- They say she used to be nice.

IF YOU COULD CHANGE ONE THING ABOUT YOUR MOM, WHAT WOULD IT BE?

- She has this weird thing about me keeping my room clean. I'd get rid of that.

- I'd make my mom smarter. Then she would know it was my sister who did it and not me.

- I would like for her to get rid of those invisible eyes on her back.

29

How Do I Love Me?

Though we need to honestly evaluate ourselves in order to grow and improve, it's easy to focus on our faults rather than our strengths. God wants us to be appropriately humble, but he doesn't want us to feed ourselves with crippling negativity. He wants us to love and respect ourselves.

In your journal or on a blank sheet of paper, make a list of positive attributes God has given to you. Don't stop until you come up with at least twelve items on your list. Then write a prayer of thanksgiving that you are wonderfully made.

If God had wanted me otherwise, he would have created me otherwise.

JOHANN VON GOETHE

Thank you for making me so wonderfully *complex!* *Your* workmanship is marvelous—and how well I *know* it.

PSALM 139:14 NLT

Dear God, My Father,

When I look at my child, my heart is filled with wonder. Even when I get impatient or irritable or even angry, I still feel so humbled to be a "mommy," to have someone to love this much.

I am amazed that you feel the same way— and so much more—about me. I am unbelievably honored that you call me your child; that you are a true daddy to me.

Today, I have a bounce in my step and a smile on my face, knowing what a wonderful father you are to me—that you created me and love me!

This is the day the Lord has made;
let us rejoice and be glad in it.

PSALM 118:24

God could not be everywhere, so he made mothers.

JEWISH PROVERB

WHAT A WONDERFUL DAY

LIFE IS WONDERFUL IN THE GOOD TIMES AND BAD TIMES.
SURE, MOTHERHOOD CAN BE TOUGH AND TAKES SOME HARD
WORK—BUT OH, THE JOYS YOU EXPERIENCE ON THE WAY.

Mother's love grows by giving.

CHARLES LAMB

The Extra Mile

When I was in college, my mother drove up one weekend to bring me home to attend my friend's wedding. As we pulled up in front of our house, I suddenly remembered I'd left the dress I planned to wear to the wedding hanging on the back of the door in my dorm room.

It was Friday evening and the stores downtown had already closed, so I couldn't go out and buy anything and I didn't have any dresses at home that I could wear.

It started to snow as we walked up the porch steps and I wailed over and over, "What am I going to do?" Mom calmly told me we'd get something to eat, and then drive back to college to get my dress.

The light snow turned into a blizzard and the drive took more than two hours each way, but my mother never once complained about having to make that extra round trip.

On that and many other occasions, my mother taught me to go the extra mile. By the way, I met my future husband at that wedding!

Your love has given me great joy and encouragement.

PHILEMON 1:7

Those who *hope*
in the Lord will
renew their strength.
They will soar
on wings like eagles;
they will run and
not grow weary,
they will walk and
not be faint.

ISAIAH 40:31

38

Rest and Renewal

"Idle hands are the devil's workshop."
Our culture values productivity more than
play and hard work more than rest.

But God not only gives us permission to
rest, he tells us that it is necessary. Moms
often have more to do in one day than most
people can do in a week!

Jesus said, "Come to me, all you who are
weary and carrying heavy burdens, and I will
give you rest" (Matthew 11:28).

It's a wonderful life when we place our
burdens into God's capable hands!

Lord, you will grant us peace, for all
we have accomplished is really from you.

ISAIAH 26:12 NLT

My grace is sufficient for you.

2 CORINTHIANS 12:9

Not every day of marriage will be filled with flowers, candlelight dinners, and romance in the air. Neither will every day of being a mother be filled with the fulfillment, joy, and charm of raising obedient, responsive, cheerful angels. Life is wonderful, but it's filled with challenges, work, and trials as well.

The good news is that we have a loving God who promises us—

- Spiritual fiber to overcome temptation: "When you are tempted, he will also provide a way out so that you can stand up under it" (1 Corinthians 10:13).

- Physical strength to face strenuous work loads: "Your sandals shall be iron and bronze; as your days, so shall your strength be (Deuteronomy 33:25, *NKJV*).

- Heavenly protection to preserve you from the attacks of Satan: "The Lord will rescue me from every evil attack and will bring me safely to his heavenly kingdom" (2 Timothy 4:18).

- Divine joy to lift your spirit in the midst of trials: "The joy of the Lord is your strength" (Nehemiah 8:10).

- Comfort and healing to bring you through grief: "He is the source of every mercy and the God who comforts us" (2 Corinthians 1:3, *NLT*).

- Sustenance to provide you with all the necessities of life: "And this same God who takes care of me will supply all your needs" (Philippians 4:19, *NLT*).

Kids Say

WHAT'S THE DIFFERENCE BETWEEN MOMS AND DADS?

- Moms work at work and work at home, and dads just go to work at work.

- Moms know how to talk to teachers without scaring them.

- Dads are taller and stronger, but moms have all the real power 'cause that's who you got to ask if you want to sleep over at your friend's.

- Moms have magic—they make you feel better without medicine.

WHAT DOES YOUR MOM DO IN HER SPARE TIME?

- Mothers don't do spare time.

- To hear her tell it, she pays bills all day long.

What's for Dinner?

One day a five-year-old declared that he was a magician and asked his younger brother what he could turn him into. The four-year-old suggested an elephant, so he said, "Abracadabra, you are an elephant!" and his brother proceeded to act like an elephant.

Then he came to his mother and said, "Mom, what can I turn you into?" His mother, who had three boys under five and was thirty-seven weeks pregnant, noted that it was almost dinnertime and responded sarcastically, "Someone who doesn't have to cook dinner!" The boy thought about it for a minute, waved his wand and said, "Abracadabra, you are Dad!"

To Do!
Balance

It is so important that we continually seek and create ways to balance work, rest, play, and worship if we are to be at our very best.

Make a list for each category—*work*, *rest*, *play*, and *worship*—of two or three things you can do in each area to better achieve balance in your life this week and in the days ahead.

If this is a major struggle area for you, you might visit a local bookstore or library and select a book on time management—or do a simple Internet search and read some free articles on keeping life in harmony. Your goal is to find one principle for each category that you can put into practice today!

To get the full benefit of this activity, plan to go to bed "on time" every night this week!

Every morning
I spend fifteen
minutes filling
my mind full of
God, and so there's
no room left for
worry thoughts.

HOWARD CHANDLER CHRISTY

Then Jesus said, "Come
to me, all of you who
are weary and carry
heavy burdens, and
I will give you rest."

MATTHEW 11:28 NLT

O Lord,

I need your help today.

*I want to care for those you've sent
into my life, to help them develop
the special gifts you've given them.
But I also want to free them to follow
their own paths and to bring their
loving wisdom to the world.*

*Help me to embrace them without clutching,
to support them without suffocating,
to correct them without crushing.*

*And help me to live joyfully and
playfully, myself, so they can see your life
in me and find their way to you.*

And now these three remain:
faith, hope and love. But
the greatest of these is love.

1 CORINTHIANS 13:13

A baby is born with a need to be loved—and never outgrows it.

FRANK A. CLARK

WHAT A WONDErFUL LoVe

YOUR LIFE BECOMES EVEN MORE WONDERFUL AS YOU EXPRESS LOVE TO THE PEOPLE IN YOUR LIFE—AND TEACH YOUR CHILDREN TO LOVE OTHERS.

Who, being loved, is poor?

OSCAR WILDE

A Real Home

She was a single mother with a five-year-old son and a ton of bills. To simply stay afloat, she rented a musty, cramped camper at a local RV park.

She was embarrassed and discouraged by her surroundings. She cringed one day as she overheard someone ask her little boy if he wished they had a real home. But her grimace was replaced with a tear—and a smile—when she heard him give this reply:

"We do have a real home; we just don't have a house to put it in."

Most of all, love each other as if your life depended on it. Love makes up for practically anything.

1 PETER 4:8 THE MESSAGE

No one has seen God, ever. But if we love one another, God dwells deeply within us, and his love becomes complete in us— perfect love!

1 JOHN 4:12 THE MESSAGE

What the World Needs Now

There are so many urgent and pressing needs in the world today.

- Work for the unemployed.
- Discipline for the indulgent.
- Goals for lost and wondering souls.
- Hope for the discouraged.
- Patience for the demanding.
- Peace for the troubled.

But the greatest need in the world today is love. And there's no better place to start spreading love than your own home.

Everybody knows that a good mother gives her children a feeling of trust and stability. She is their earth. She is the one they can count on for the things that matter most of all. She is their food and their bed and the extra blanket when it grows cold in the night; she is their warmth and their health and their shelter; she is the one they want to be near when they cry. She is the only person in the whole world in a whole lifetime who can be these things to her children. There is no substitute for her. Somehow even her clothes feel different to her children's hands from anybody else's clothes. Only to touch her skirt or her sleeve makes a troubled child feel better.

KATHARINE BUTLER HATHAWAY

*Love is patient and kind. Love
is not jealous or boastful or proud
or rude. Love does not demand its
own way. Love is not irritable, and it
keeps no record of when it has been
wronged. It is never glad about
injustice but rejoices whenever the
truth wins out. Love never gives up,
never loses faith, is always
hopeful, and endures through
every circumstance.*

1 CORINTHIANS 13:4-7 NLT

Four Hugs a Day

We all need to feel loved. Some scientists estimate a minimum of four hugs a day as necessary for survival, eight for maintenance, and twelve for growth.

One study showed that ten minutes of handholding with a romantic partner can dramatically reduce a high stress level. Participating couples were divided into two groups and asked to watch a ten-minute video and discuss the way it made them feel. Couples in Group A were allowed to hold hands during the video and then asked to hug for twenty seconds afterward. Couples in Group B could not touch during or after the video.

Group B was found to have a higher heart rate and blood pressure, while Group A showed signs of being physiologically relaxed. The study also showed that positive touch causes changes in blood chemistry—lowering stress hormones and boosting "feel good" chemicals in the brain.

Make sure you hug the people you care about— their health may depend on it!

Love is what binds us all together in perfect harmony.

COLOSSIANS 3:14 NLT

A Date Day

Children spell "love" a little differently than adults: T - I - M- E.

Plan an age-appropriate, kid-friendly "date" with your child for sometime in the next week. Don't rush the experience with strict time constraints, but savor every moment. If your child is younger, take him or her to a kid's movie or plan a park outing. If you have a teen, go shopping or out to lunch—or whatever you know they would love to do.

Outings are
so much fun
when we can
savor them
through the
children's eyes.

LAWANA BLACKWELL

Family Portraits

Teacher Debbie Moon's first graders were discussing a picture of a family. One little boy in the picture had a different hair color than the other family members. One child suggested that he was adopted

A little girl excitedly wiggled her hand and exclaimed, "I know all about adoptions because I was adopted!"

"What does it mean to be adopted?" asked another child.

"It means," said the girl, "that you grew in your mommy's heart instead of her tummy."

Heavenly Father,

*I can't imagine a greater love than the love
a mother has for her children; the love that
I have for my children! No wonder they look
first to me for comfort when they are hurt.
But Father, your infinite loving-kindness is
far beyond the finite love I can give to my
children. Your comfort reaches all the way
to the depths of my soul, reviving my spirit.
Whenever I feel that I am giving more than
I am receiving in life, I will remember the
everlasting love you lavish upon me.
You are my Father God. And you love
me as tenderly as a mother!*

Children are a gift from the Lord;
they are a reward from him.

PSALM 127:3 NLT

The only thing worth stealing is a kiss from a sleeping child.

JOE HOULDSWORTH

WHAT A WONDERFUL GIFT

MARY WAS VISITED BY AN ANGEL AND TOLD THAT SHE
WOULD CARRY GOD'S SON. BUT EVEN WITHOUT A VISIT FROM
AN ANGEL, EVERY MOTHER KNOWS HER CHILD IS A SPECIAL GIFT.

Help us to be the always hopeful gardeners of the spirit who know that without darkness nothing comes to birth as without light nothing flowers.

MAY SARTON

Wildflowers

The young mother sat staring out the window. She had spent most of the day alone and longed for the school bell to ring. Suddenly, she saw her daughter, Becky, running across the field toward home.

The mom jumped up and ran to the door to welcome her. When she opened the door Becky stood there with a smile on her face and holding a fistful of wildflowers.

"These are for you, Mama!" she shouted.

After she hugged Becky and swung her in a circle in the air, the mom pulled out a glass, filled it with water, and placed the tiny bouquet in the middle of the dining room table.

Some people may have seen the floral arrangement as a fistful of weeds, but her mother saw them as a perfect centerpiece, a smile from the heart.

So we praise God for the wonderful kindness he has poured out on us because we belong to his dearly loved Son.

EPHESIANS 1:6 NLT

We worry about
what a child will
become tomorrow,
yet we forget
that he is
someone today.

STACIA TAUSCHER

A Fresh Perspective

Twin girls were separated at birth and adopted. One mother sulked that the baby girl would not eat unless she put cinnamon on her food. The other mother happily reported how easy it was to feed her baby just by putting cinnamon on all her food.

Sometimes we make being a mother harder than it should be by the way we think about things. We obsess over past mistakes and worries of the future. But when we enjoy our children, appreciate our children, we begin to experience a more profound joy in our parenting.

There is no such thing as perfect parenting, but living in the moment, being grateful for the gift of each day, will greatly benefit us as we seek to lovingly relate to our children. The fresh perspective of allowing ourselves to enjoy our children will foster their self-esteem—and rekindle the joy of motherhood.

Finally, brothers, whatever is true, whatever is noble, whatever is right, whatever is pure, whatever is lovely, whatever is admirable—if anything is excellent or praiseworthy—think about such things.

PHILIPPIANS 4:8

Hannah's Gift

*He gives childless couples
a family, gives them joy as the
parents of children. Hallelujah!*

PSALM 113:9 THE MESSAGE

One of the most beautiful stories of a mother's love in the Bible is that of Hannah.

Her heart's desire was to have a child, but after years of marriage, it did not appear that she was physically able to get pregnant. The grief she felt was deep, but was made even worse by the way she was treated by her husband's other wife. In this day when polygamy was still the norm, it was the wife who bore the most children who was often most revered.

In abject grief, Hannah visited the temple and poured out her heart to God. Her crying was so intense that the priest on duty scolded her for being drunk. When she told him the burden of her heart, he prophetically replied back to her, "May the God of Israel grant the request you have asked of him" (1 Samuel 1:17, *NLT*).

Hannah did have a son. She named him Samuel, which means "asked of God." And true to her word, she offered Samuel back to God with a profound sense of gratitude and an absolute confidence that he was a gift from God. She brought him to the temple where he served God and later became the chief priest of his nation.

You may not be asked to offer your child in service to the church—though perhaps God will call him or her to ministry—but all of us are asked to trust God with our most precious gifts, even our children.

Every beetle is a gazelle in the eyes of its mother.

MOORISH PROVERB

Precious, Precocious Children

Every mother instinctively knows that her child is special. Are there any children more precious and precocious than yours?

Mothers in the animal kingdom understand this as well. Consider the mother of a healthy blue whale calf. The baby can swim the moment she is born, rising unaided to the surface of the ocean to take her first breath. The calf will double her weight in the first week, eventually tipping the scales at 150 tons.

Unless you have a growing teenage boy, your children won't grow that fast. But isn't it wonderful to watch their lives develop and unfold?

What a pleasure it is to have wise children.

PROVERBS 23:24 NLT

Life Is a Gift

One of the lost arts of civility and friendship is the handwritten note. Take time today to write several thank-you notes. Write notes to your spouse, your own parents, friends who have been an encouragement to you, and yes, even a handwritten note to your child!

God gave you
a gift of 86,400
seconds today.
Have you used
one to say
"thank you"?

WILLIAM A. WARD

My Greatest Achievement

Watching my baby grow and do new things makes me so proud. The first time he rolled over, I started crying. When he is laughing and happy, my eyes well up and I feel so full of love and so proud of him. It makes me wonder what I would ever do without him. Becoming a mother brings such a deep emotional connection, and I think it is the greatest achievement and most amazing gift in my life.

I prayed for this child, and the Lord has granted me what I asked of him. So now I give him to the Lord. For his whole life he will be given over to the Lord.

1 SAMUEL 1:27, 28

Dear Heavenly Father,

Thank you for the gift of my children.
I'm grateful, God, for every laugh and hug, for
the privilege of sharing in their accomplishments,
for the love they bring to my life.

God, I'm amazed that you've entrusted to me
these precious lives. Lord, I give them over
to you and pray that you would guide each day
of their lives. Thank you for the opportunity to
help them grow into strong young people who
love you. Please give me wisdom to share
and daily gratitude for this amazing gift.

I know what I'm doing. I have it all planned out—
plans to take care of you, not abandon you,
plans to give you the future you hope for.

JEREMIAH 29:11 THE MESSAGE

Everyone's future is, in reality, uncertain and full of unknown treasures from which all may draw unguessed prizes.

LORD DUNSANY

WHAT A WONDERFUL TOMORROW

LIFE IS WONDERFUL TODAY—BECAUSE WE ALSO HAVE THE HOPE OF WONDERFUL TOMORROWS. OUR KIDS WILL GROW AND MATURE—AND GOD IS STILL WORKING ON YOU AS WELL!

Let your faith in Christ be in the quiet confidence that he will every day and every moment keep you as the apple of his eye, keep you in perfect peace and in the sure experience of all the light and strength you need.

ANDREW MURRAY

Never Alone

She needed to spend a few days alone. Her business had kept her busy. She had what seemed like hundreds of deadlines to meet. Her husband had been occupied with his job. She realized that she needed some time away from busyness to talk to God and stretch her spirit.

She packed her bags and went to the beach. She missed her husband almost before she got out of the car—she couldn't remember the last time she took a trip without him. She felt lonely.

The first morning there, she awoke early enough to greet the sun as it rose over the ocean. The rising sun became a perfect backdrop as a cloud took the shape of a cross. She knew then that she wasn't alone at all. She had come to the beach to meet God and grow—and he had met her there.

And I am sure that God, who began the good work within you, will continue his work until it is finally finished on that day when Christ Jesus comes back again.

PHILIPPIANS 1:6 NLT

A Bright Future

My purpose is to give life in all its fullness.
JOHN 10:10 NLT

Life doesn't feel wonderful when we allow the clouds of fear and doubt to trouble our hearts. The good news is that God secures our future—

- He replaces uncertainty with the promise of good days (Jeremiah 29:11).
- He provides peace in the midst of storms (John 14:27).
- He hears our prayers (1 John 5:14).
- He quells worry with his peace (Philippians 4:7).
- He promises us an eternal home (Revelation 21:3).

Smile. Trust God for your—and your child's—future.

Life is God's novel. Let him write it.

ISAAC BASHEVIS
SINGER

I am not afraid
of tomorrow,
for I have seen
yesterday and
I love today.

WILLIAM ALLEN WHITE

I will not
leave you as
orphans;
I will come
to you.

JOHN 14:18

A Wonderful Goal

People who articulate their dreams, goals, and plans tend to be more successful at achieving desired results and feeling a sense of purpose.

What are some of the dreams and goals you have for your life? How can you help instill a sense of purpose in the lives of your children? Write down four or five major goals for your life. Under each goal, write down three or four very specific action steps. It would be great if at least one of the goals was something that could be accomplished in the next year, and one of the goals should be something that might take a number of years.

If your children are in their teen years, work with them on doing the same activity for themselves.

If you have young school-age children, try a very directed activity of helping them state one very specific and attainable "future" goal—i.e. a new bike—and give them a few tasks to help achieve that goal.

There is one thing that gives radiance to everything. It is the idea of something around the corner.

G. K. CHESTERTON

As a mother comforts her child, so will I comfort you.

ISAIAH 66:13

God pardons like a mother who kisses away the repentant tears of her child.

HENRY WARD BEECHER

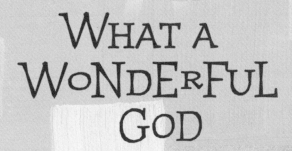

WHAT A WONDERFUL GOD

Life is wonderful because God created it that way. He's the giver of all good gifts—including your children.

I would rather walk with God in the dark than go alone in the light.

MARY GARDINER BRAINARD

God's Light

A mother and her four-year-old daughter were preparing for bed one night. The child was afraid of the dark, and the mother, on this occasion, felt fearful also.

When the light was out, the child caught a glimpse of the moon outside the window. "Mother," she asked, "is the moon God's light?" "Yes," said the mother.

The next question was, "Will God put out his light and go to sleep?" The mother replied, "No, my child, God never goes to sleep."

Then out of the simplicity of a child's faith, she said these words which gave reassurance to the fearful mother: "Well, as long as God's light is on, he's awake, and we might as well go to sleep."

The Lord keeps watch over you as you
come and go, both now and forever.

PSALM 121:8 NLT

For he, the Mighty One, is holy, and he has done great things for me. His mercy goes on from generation to generation, to all who fear him.

LUKE 1:49, 50 NLT

Lessons from the Life of Mary

Mary, the mother of Jesus, is perhaps the best known of all the women of the Bible. People across the world know her name and honor her.

Mary was an ordinary young woman—until the day an angel suddenly appeared and said, "Greetings, you who are highly favored! The Lord is with you" (Luke 1:28). The angel told her that she had been chosen to carry Jesus, the Savior of the world.

Mary could have questioned and fretted over this news. But she simply said yes to God's plan: "May it be to me as you have said" (Luke 1:38). She placed her reputation, her marriage, and her entire life at risk to be obedient to God—and trusted that his will was perfect.

And because of her love for and obedience to God, salvation became available to all humanity.

Mary's heartfelt trust in God and readiness to do his will brought the blessing of God into her life.

To Do!

Count Your Blessings

What do you have to be thankful to God for? Make a list of God's blessings in the last week, month, and year (for example: your children and husband, meeting your material needs, lifting your spirits at opportune times). Then write a note of thanks to God and tuck it in your Bible for future reference.

Gratitude is happiness doubled by wonder.

G.K. CHESTERTON

Thank God for his Son— a gift too wonderful for words!

2 CORINTHIANS 9:15 NLT

Dear Lord,

Because of your Spirit within me,
I am a person of gratitude! I refuse
to take my blessings for granted; to
complain about petty annoyances
and inconveniences; to focus on what
I don't have when I live in a land of
plenty; to grumble and gossip when
there is so much positive to see
and say. Today, Lord, I say to
you, thank you, thank you,
thank you, thank you!

A Prayer for a Mother's Heart

*If God cares so wonderfully for flowers that are here today
and gone tomorrow, won't he more surely care for you?*

MATTHEW 6:30 NLT

Dear Heavenly Father,

*I can get so caught up in my needs and problems that I
sometimes forget that you are the giver of all good gifts
and that you know—and meet all my needs.*

*I know that I don't have all the answers, but I choose to
live with confidence and faith because you promise to
give me exactly what I need each day.*

Amen.